TEN NORTH-EAST POETS

TEN NORTH-EAST POETS

an anthology edited by
NEIL ASTLEY

BLOODAXE
BOOKS

ISBN: 0 906427 13 4

First published 1980 by
Bloodaxe Books
1 North Jesmond Avenue
Jesmond
Newcastle upon Tyne
NE2 3JX

The publisher acknowledges the financial assistance of Northern Arts

Typesetting by Graphic Design Workshop, Newcastle upon Tyne

Printed in Great Britain by
Unwin Brothers Limited, Old Woking, Surrey

for Tony Harrison,
from some of his readers

CONTENTS

PREFACE

In 1966, shortly after its move to Newcastle, *Stand* magazine (8 no. 2) published a survey of contemporary writing in North-East England. The editors' conclusions, given in an article by Rodney Pybus, were that most of the work by new writers submitted for the 'regional writing' issue was 'worse than third-rate . . . abysmal'; the exceptions were Tom Pickard, Barry MacSweeney, and the dialect poet Fred Reed.

The *Stand* survey presented 'a depressing picture of the region's literary talent'; the outlook, moreover, was said to be 'bleak'. But much has happened in the North-East since 1966: several important poets have established or consolidated their reputations; and there are also a number of talented new writers whose work is not yet widely known. The ten North-East poets of this selection have previously only been published in magazines, anthologies and pamphlets. They do not comprise a group, nor do they hold any common poetic allegiance; indeed, their only link is in being published here together. But they do share a freshness of approach to their craft which invigorates whatever style each has chosen to develop. It is my hope that this anthology will introduce their work to a wider readership. Three of them have collections of different kinds published by or forthcoming from Bloodaxe Books, and their selections here are mainly of other poems. Any consideration of their work should also take account of those collections: David Constantine's first book, *A Brightness to Cast Shadows*; Vincent Morrison's pamphlet, *The Season of Comfort*; and Stephen Dunstan's *Tarot Poems*, his first publication (as well as his forthcoming book of translations of the Chinese poet Ma Zhi-yuan).

In order to place the poets of this anthology in some kind of context, I shall attempt some updating of Pybus's essay—which is still the best historical account of the literature of North-East England. The only other guide to contemporary poetry in the North-East has been William Parkinson's contribution to the critical anthology *British Poetry since 1960* (Carcanet, 1972). This negative, didactic essay is unbalanced, in particular, by over-long, heavy-handed attacks on Pickard and MacSweeney, via Basil Bunting; it ends, however, on an uncharacteristic note of optimism:

> It is as well that Jon Silkin and Tony Harrison are now living and working in the region; their presence, and the *Stand* quarterly now published in

> Newcastle, may well influence and encourage the next generation of poets. . . We can hope that [they] will find the means to express the impulse and experience of their region and produce a literature of repute, based on the best of folk tradition and continuing the high-level of achievement represented by the novels of Sid Chaplin . . .

But these, I shall argue, are two separate issues—sometimes complementary, sometimes not.

It should be possible now to consider the influence of Harrison, Silkin, and *Stand*. Tony Harrison's work has presented an inspiring example: its technical virtuosity, classical precision and colloquial vigour are so unified that the poet's tone and voice are exact, individual and unaffected. This alone would be a rare achievement nowadays, yet Harrison has sought not only to master the difficult mode of poetry but also to make it embody and serve his own cause. He has refused to detach himself from a world which would frustrate the artist's attempt to articulate its contradictions; in this he is isolated, but not removed, for he voices both his own alienation and that of the working class, and, moreover, that of any disowned or repressed individual or people. That Harrison is a major poet has long been recognised, by poets; his poems from *The School of Eloquence* (Rex Collings, 1978), a continuing sequence, were said by Jeffrey Wainwright to 'speak of our culture in a way that makes them some of the most important poems of the present day' (*Poetry Review,* 69 no.1 [1979]).

To have had a poet of Harrison's stature living in Newcastle has, I believe, encouraged many writers in the North-East, not least those represented in this anthology; but because he has in recent years mainly lived and worked in London and abroad, they have missed the stimulating readings, and magazine appearances of new poems have therefore assumed a special importance (it is fortunate in this respect that many are published in *Stand*). I do not, however, find much evidence of direct poetic influence, either by Harrison or by Silkin, in the mature work of the new North-East writers; on the whole it has been a case of influence by example rather than through uncritical stylistic modelling. Harrison has shown ways of exploring concerns that are vitally felt in the North-East: how to express what Parkinson called the region's 'impulse and experience' with complete openness; how to balance what is salvagable and still relevant in 'folk tradition' with what the national and international culture have to offer. In Silkin's case, his editing of *Stand* (with its programme of committed art) has, I feel, been more influential than his poetry. The presence of an international literary magazine is particularly stimulating in an area not noted for broad-mindedness; but the North-East also nurtures a fierce spirit of independence, and this, paradoxically, fuels a drive for openness in the regional culture.

William Parkinson complained that modern poets in the North-East had lost the 'close creative relationship' with their communities which the nineteenth-century pitman-poets had drawn upon for their songs. The oral tradition, however, was a local phenomenon—or 'parochial', to use the word, complimentarily, in Patrick Kavanagh's sense of the writer who 'is never in any doubt about the social and artistic validity of his parish'. This is a question of belief: Kavanagh's commitment was rooted in Monaghan, his kingdom of 'banks and stones and every blooming thing' ('Inniskeen Road: July Evening'), its boundaries fixed eternally by 'incurious' black hills ('Shancoduff'). Tarry Flynn, Kavanagh tells us, is 'not a country man, but a man living. And life was the same everywhere'. In the hands of a writer of genius, the intimately known local world becomes a microcosm; in 'Epic', a poem about a dispute over the ownership of 'half a rood of rock', Homer's "ghost" whispers: 'I made the Iliad from such/A local row . . . ' However, Kavanagh's definition of the 'parochial' writer (often quoted outside its Irish context by defenders of "regionalism") characterises a 'mentality' which undoubtedly *was* a positive source of strength to poets like Kavanagh, or William Barnes—just as religion had been for Herbert and Hopkins—but which could as easily be applied to the dull verses of a country parson, or those of a "local poet". Nor are such certainities as Kavanagh expresses so likely to be found now, except as negatives; or as a sign of immature obtuseness.

Parkinson's attack on those North-East poets who, 'standing apart from their communities . . . are prone to the self-regarding excesses of an illusory idealism', displays a confused, anachronistic and doctrinaire view of poetry; it is, moreover, inconsistent both with his praise of Douglas Dunn's *Terry Street* (Faber, 1969)—'[Dunn] is aware of the gulf between himself and the people of the street and uses this separateness to give us a sense of himself and them . . . '—and with the reality of Dunn's 'creative relationship' with the Terry Street community. '*Terry Street*,' says Parkinson, 'gives a rare sense of the quality of working-class life'; Dunn sees it differently: 'I was offended by their complacency: that is, towards the environment . . . I found the people infected by popular culture' (*London Magazine*, 19 no.8 [1979]). While that is a later reassessment, it is in no sense a re-writing; Dunn is sympathetic towards the people in most of the poems, but those which seek to show 'the country as a whole' (*ibid.*) through Terry Street focus his disillusionment and anger at the way their common culture has been debased or destroyed by the modern diseases of commercialisation and political self-interest (poems like 'The Clothes Pit', 'Young Women in Rollers', and, particularly, 'The Silences'). Dunn has become an outsider, standing apart from a working-class community whose values are no longer adequate, and which cannot be shared; his subject-matter may often be regional—life in Hull or his native Clydeside—but his concerns are wider. 'Poetry,' he has said, 'is a larger concept than nationalism or a national idea of poetry' (*Aquarius* 11 [1979]); and this, of course, is even more true of a regional idea of poetry.

The alternative is a prescription for minor art. To concentrate on specifically local, social or contemporary issues is to narrow one's perspective to that of a "local writer", a political spokesman or a journalist. These limitations indeed characterise the work of the North-East's self-proclaimed "local writers"; the Tyneside Poets (who publish the magazine *Poetry North East*) maintain the poor standards noted in Pybus's account of 1966: little of their work is distinguishable, rhythmically, from prose, and much of it consists of sentimental journalism or jokey autobiography (traits typical also of the prose of "local writers").

When *Stand* was looking for signs of 'a strong regional consciousness' in the work of new writers living in the North-East, how narrow was that definition? How central to a writer's work is his 'regional consciousness'? I'm heartened by what Jon Silkin has said about 'genuinely regional literature' since then; he has found 'an abrasive vitality in the North', and in Tom Pickard's first book, *High on the Walls* (Fulcrum, 1967), 'a sort of stubbornness and recalcitrance that I would associate with the Northern experience' ('The Small Magazine since 1960—a recorded conversation with Jon Silkin', *British Poetry since 1960*). Silkin's North is composite, including the various landscapes and communities of Tyneside, Co. Durham, Northumberland, and Leeds, his previous home; and Bunting's Northumbria is the old kingdom, stretching from the Humber up to the Tweed and to the west across the Pennines. William Parkinson, who believes that a distinctive regional voice is lacking in the poetry of Pickard, MacSweeney and Bunting, does find it in 'the work of the immigrants like Jon Silkin and Tony Harrison'; yet that 'abrasive vitality' is, as Silkin says, of the North—in Harrison's case, one can find it both in his poems about the North-East and in those about his childhood in Leeds. But this is still too narrow an approach. Silkin's *Killhope Wheel* poems (MidNAG, 1971; *The Principle of Water* [Carcanet, 1974]) express a deep-rooted historical sympathy with the struggle of the individual against poverty and exploitation in the industrial North-East; it is the first time that he has been able to identify himself with the region. While he has written much since about Northumberland, his indignation has not on the whole been so sharply focussed on the outrageous social conditions that the North-East has lived through; yet he has written about the persecution of the Jews in Jerusalem and in medieval York, about love, death, grief, oppression, torture, brutality—in short, about being 'a man living'—and the Northern experience, while inseparable from his identity, is but one aspect of it.

What I have been describing is surely committed art in its broadest and most proper sense. We can consider particular concerns—with work by Silkin or work published by him in *Stand* serving as examples—and find other poets in the North-East exploring similar areas. The historical struggle in *Killhope Wheel* must have helped other poets focus their responses to the North-East, and one wonders if it didn't show the way for poems like James Longwill's 'Bobby Arnct' (see below, p.74). Jeffrey Wainwright's poems about life during the Industrial Revolution—for example '1815', first published in *Stand* in 1968 (*The Important Man* [Northern House, 1970]; *Heart's Desire* [Carcanet, 1978])—show a more restrained approach which may also have been instructive. While such poems help define the Northern experience, their basic concerns are wider; moreover, *Stand*'s internationalism provides a valuable perspective: a common chord is struck, for instance, by poets writing about the oppressive conditions of life in Eastern Europe, the Soviet Union, and parts of Africa and Latin America.

Many small presses and little magazines exist to publish particularly narrow areas; and they do a good job in providing a platform for poets who share their limited concerns. Yet too often their advocates will proclaim a certain approach to be the only valid concept of poetry; it seems to me that these "small critics" (why not give them the same adjective?) *expect* small presses to serve only these small areas—in particular, experimental and political writing. The most prominent of the small critics is now Jeff

Nuttall, whose monthly reviews of small press publications in *The Guardian* concentrate almost exclusively on experimental poetry; his arguments are not unflawed:

> The pressure is such amongst the crowded readings and the hastily duplicated pages that a poet needs far more to register his professional identity in 1979 than the ability to say something special nicely. Conventional articulacy and the heart's truth are all very well but the poets who emerge as the most rewarding from the seething literary scene are those who are aware that poetry is first of all made of words and that words are first of all made of breath, sound, time, ink, space and paper before they start to function as the bearers of dictionary meanings. [*The Guardian*, 14 July 1979]

Such sophistry would be offensive if it weren't so patently absurd. It is a typical example of the small criticism (when did poetry *ever* serve merely to 'say something special nicely'?). The Nuttall alternative to craft and feeling is this slapdash prescription for knocking up "poems" out of breath, ink, and the other things, a recipe which is indeed followed by many of the writers whom he praises (extravagantly) in his columns. And *these* are our 'most rewarding' poets?

Reviewing the pamphlet *The Season of Comfort*, Jim Burns criticised Vincent Morrison for 'backing off from the contemporary' (*Ambit* 79 [1979]); to write about the past, or about Nature, is to 'ignore the fact [sic] that standing on a street corner in a sea of broken glass might be more typical of the times we live in'. I'm reminded here of Randall Jarrell's observation that 'a kind of nauseated brutality (in which the writer's main response to the world is simply to vomit) will seem to many critics and readers the inescapable truth' ('Poets, Critics, and Readers'). Fortunately, Burns' sea of broken of glass is neither wholly typical nor inescapable, and nor can it symbolise anything more than a fraction of human experience in the present day. I do not believe that one can possibly adopt this kind of street corner vantage-point and still write with authority.

Edward Lucie-Smith, in the Penguin anthology *British Poetry since 1945* (1970), categorised poetry in Newcastle as 'post-Poundian', alluding to the presence of Basil Bunting and to the group of young poets then associated with him and with the Morden Tower—in particular Tom Pickard and Barry MacSweeney. Long before Bunting's reputation was properly established in Britain, with the publication in 1966 of *Briggflatts* (by Fulcrum Press), he had a strong following in the States among the avant-garde, the experimental writers, the Beat poets, the Black Mountain "school"; the American poets (like Creeley and Ginsberg) came to Newcastle to see Bunting, and to read at the Morden Tower, then enjoying its heyday as an important centre for the new popular poetry. The younger poets were not only reading Bunting and Pound (and Zukofsky), but were also discovering this new American poetry, little of which was then widely available in Britain; but small presses like Fulcrum, Trigram, Migrant and Grosseteste were publishing the poetry of the English and American avant-garde (including Pickard and MacSweeney). The 'post-Poundian' group in the North-East has been well served by its own presses: the Morden Tower imprint and MacSweeney's Black Suede Boot Press (now in Folkestone), and later Brian Marley's Laundering Room Press and the now flourishing Pig Press run by Ric Caddel; recently Peter Hodgkiss brought *Poetry Information* (replaced by *Not Poetry*) and Galloping Dog Press to Newcastle, and Colin Simms's Genera Editions is now also Newcastle-based.

This strong local tradition of experimental/avant-garde writing is also something of a millstone. When this anthology was first advertised, I was attacked by Yann Lovelock, reviews editor of *Iron* magazine, for claiming that it would 'dispose of the notion that the departure of Tom Pickard left the North-East devoid of talented young writers'. 'Now, as things go,' I was told, 'poets like Koef Nielsen, Brian Marley, Tony Jackson, Ric Caddel, are generally reckoned to be the heirs of the departed and to share roughly the same ground as them.' I don't dispute that the work of these writers is similar in approach to that of Pickard and MacSweeney, and I would not presume to deprecate their poetry (some of which is very fine); but they are the 'heirs' only in continuing that same line. My intention was to publish the best of the North-East's new generation of poets, and this I would maintain I have done; in my view, most of the poetry which appears in this anthology is more significant than that of the writers whom Lovelock commends (all of whom have in any case been much more widely published in the little magazines and by the presses listed above). Lovelock accuses me of 'ignoring the experimental side and sticking mainly to safe traditionalists'; yet the anthology selection is quite wide-ranging, reflecting a catholicity which I hope is evident also in the Bloodaxe list as a whole. The phrase 'safe traditionalists' is pure jargon; one has presumably to exclude from it Eliot's 'historical sense' of tradition (which is anything but 'safe'), and to interpret it instead as the standard jibe against 'traditional' styles or modes of expression; one's 'traditional' sense of rhythm, form, sound, syntax, tone, may have been developed by poets over several centuries, but— according to the spokesmen of the avant-garde—*the pressures of life today* are such that 'traditional' poetry is now obsolete, tired, tame, academic, middle-class, irrelevant, etc. The confused liaison between modern poetry and pop culture during the 60s may have encouraged such fallacies. Of course popular writing is not necessarily significant, and often it is ephemeral (*vide* Michael Horovitz's *Children of Albion* 'underground' anthology); with its audience reduced to a (vocal) clique, the claims of the avant-garde now look rather inflated; and their pretence of authority shows an unintelligent lack of perspective.

In conclusion, I would argue that Patrick Kavanagh's view of regional poetry is oversimple; and that in the North-East the best poets are neither inward-looking nor stand-offish. The North-East's literary tradition has become not folk-based but international in outlook. It seems to me not coincidental that several poets are also distinguished translators, notably Bunting, Harrison, Alistair Elliot, and Fleur Adcock, the current Northern Arts Literary Fellow (all four are classicists); Jon Silkin too has done translations, collaborating recently with his fellow editor David McDuff, another accomplished poet-translator. Poetry in the North-East must not be separated from its national context; the "experimental" group is part of the present avant-garde, while the more important poets are contributing to the mainstream of English poetry. Any consideration of contemporary poetry in the North-East should concentrate on the latter area, and in particular on the work of Tony Harrison, Jon Silkin, Rodney Pybus, Richard Kell and Alistair Elliot. I would like to suggest that some of the poets in this anthology could be seen as extending that tradition.

NEIL ASTLEY

ACKNOWLEDGEMENTS

Some of these poems have appeared in the following publications:

PETER ARMSTRONG: *Passing Through* (Sunderland Polytechnic), *Poetry Review.*

GEORGE CHARLTON: *Bananas*, *The Blue Lion* (Newcastle University), *Caret*, *London Magazine*, *Meridian*, *New Poetry 2* (Arts Council, 1976), *Stand.*

DAVID CONSTANTINE: *Poetry Review.* The first five poems appear in his book *A Brightness to Cast Shadows* (Bloodaxe Books, 1980).

DESMOND GRAHAM: *Bananas*, *The Blue Lion* (Newcastle University), *Dragoncards 7* (Mandeville Press).

JAMES LONGWILL: *Iron*, *New Blackfriars*, *New Poetry 5* (Hutchinson/Arts Council—P.E.N., 1979), *Stand.* The first two poems appeared in his pamphlet *A Man's Jacket* (Pig Press, 1977).

VINCENT MORRISON: *Iron*, *New Poetry 2* (Arts Council, 1976), *Poetry North East*, *Stand*, *Two Poets and an Illustrator* (Wearmouth 1300 Festival, 1974). The first three poems appear in his pamphlet *The Season of Comfort* (Bloodaxe Books, 1979).

LAWRIE WALKER: *Poetry Review*, *Stand.*

MIKE WILKIN: *The Honest Ulsterman*, *Iron.*

I should like to thank Roger Garfitt for his help; Yann Lovelock for allowing me to quote from a letter in the Preface; and Graham Smith of Amber Films (9 The Side, Newcastle upon Tyne NE1 3JE) for the cover photograph. Special thanks are due to Northern Arts for the generous support given to this anthology and other publications. N.A.

PETER ARMSTRONG

Silent Ancestry

1. *At the lake head*

The path clags
underfoot, a snare
of fern, trickster
in the reed-bed.

I have come silent-footed
through firs, on paths
matted with the years'
shed needles

and stand barefoot,
my toes curled
in the humus
at the wood's edge.

2. *Schism*

I am cumber-footed
in these sepia
presences, dark-faced
generations lined

before me, the slow
exposure of mind,
a silent ancestry

men who worked steel
who crossed from Ireland
sure-footed, Catholic.

Another Company

We are drunk
with Malory –

beguiled by Scott
and Spenser.

An ill-focused age
glimmers

the image
never sharpens

beyond
Coeur-de-Lion.

But now
I see another company

stragglers
from their masters' wars

barely visible
above the skyline.

The foreground
diminishes –

the lists
are abandoned

to that grey
column

that does not
advance.

Tollesbury

Here the lines are indistinct;
the sky, the sea
the Essex marshes

where the fleet

once bore the grain
in barges, from Old Hall
down to the Blackwater
and the Thames

where the cowbell clatter
of halliard on mast
rattles against
the wind.

Land peters into sea;
the broad fingering estuaries
dovetail mud.

Wind rises, and shifts

bearing from land
the smoke of stubble.

At Evening

Now only wind –
the first leaf falls
in the beginnings of rain,

and seaward
the tide shifts,
bares the mud

a rib of rotten hull.

*

One works late;
pauses to note
the day seep
under the hedges

while far up
a vapour trail
catches the light
and is nearly blinding.

'All day north'

All day north, this business
of harvest.
            Here, cresting
the Tees' hummocking watershed,
the harvester's shadow
falls on wheat.

Two hundred miles
have made close on
a season's difference;

south, the stubble
turned into furrow.

'At the field's corner'

At the field's corner,

shabby, tired
they stand.

The evening wind
chills their sweat

curls and eddies
the last standing wheat.

Arden great moor
rises from the vale,

and then
forty miles of moor
to the sea;

heather ruffled
by the omnipotent wind
from Hasty Bank
to Fylingdales.

These men are small,
stood by their skew-parked cars,
a season's work
completed;

too near
that bald rim
to convince.

Artesian

The ground is cracked
that was rich loam;
brittle that mashed well
in the farmer's hand.

He cups dust.
Wind scoops dust
from the river-cliff, lets fall
a dry precipitation

on stony fields. Seeds
lie stiff, knotted,
infertile as stone: light
bare of water

raises no crop. And now
he must drill deep
to where the winter's rain
lies wombed in stone;

already he pictures
the germ swell and burst,
the shoot nuzzle toward light
through dark earth.

He treads home across
pale soil, the powdered furrow
that will cling this winter
to his step.

'The shack's chawn timbers'

The shack's chawn timbers
flake. The wind
is tubercular
in flooring crevices.

Scrag cattle mill
at dry water holes
nuzzle the once-claggy earth
hollow-socketed, stupid

with drought. Sand's
fluid motion has doused
a border farm;
left cropless

and corpse-cattled
an émigré's first holding;
and the track
is barely rutted

that he has walked
toward a new hinterland.
The wind is blowing
billowing of black

in that interior
to which creeps
the insidious tide
of sand.

Plain Kate

Webs thread
light. A cracked porthole
split this spectrum
on the cabin wall
shafted dust's
quiet suspension.

She rests
where the creek
has wound, measuring
each rise, each lull of tide
against a wharf
green with tides.

It is a last anchorage.

A much flooded path
comes here and a creek
often mud.
                    Below deck
a sprig of samphire
rests on the table. Touch
and it crumbles.

'Footprints'

Footprints
                    deft impressions
of leaving, traced in dew
across tussocked grass.

Growth runs ruinous
falls
sifts into humus.

Autumn descends
in fog.

November
                and the hoar-frost
stiffens grass. The beech-hedge
holds its last brittle leaves

has littered a border with those fallen.

Dawn is as grey as breath.
Only the rose presents
a clear outline

of thorn.

The Remaining

Three cygnets I saw,
late in the year
and parentless
on Crag Lough,
the valley barred
by basalt walls
and flightless wings.

GEORGE CHARLTON

Night Shift Workers

They have come from a factory
Where fluorescent strips flared all night

And ears grew numb to machinery;
They are going home to working wives,

To cooling beds at breakfast time,
Undressing fatigue from their skin like clothes;

Later to wake at four and taste teeth
Soft as fur in their mouths.

They live in a dislocation of hours
Inside-out like socks pulled on in darkness

Waking when the day is over.
They are always at an ebb, unlike others

Going out to work in the morning
Where sun and moon shine in the sky together.

Sea Coal

This is the coal-coast. Where Seaham tilts seawards
Splintered suns float on the North Sea's pressure
Compounding best coal squeezed from strata

Between seafloor and rock bed. Below,
Sunken eyes lie back exhausted;
Cold currents unpick the sinews of men

Who rippled in earnest coaling Imperial flotillas:
Both bone-cage and bulkhead fronds
Have fossilised in sea-salt.

Underwater siftings are washing
From the stokehold of the sea, poor nuts,
For sea coal burns badly, gives off meagre heat.

It has become derelict treasure salvaged
Out of an undertow. Coal has produced
Its own decay: coal-pickers who scrounge

Bent-backed on the water fringe balance
Sacks on the cross-bars of clapped out bikes,
Stretch their spines and look out, gazing –

There dead things have come from the sea to tell
Bleached tales to the hard-up and out of work,
Rumouring of desolation riding the slack.

Friday Evenings

The evening star sparks
Struck like a welding arc.

In dull light of the varnished pubs
Young men wait, scrubbed clean as water babies,

A faint idea of work dismissed
And leisure compromised.

Here and there a moustache soft as lichen
Moistens on the white head of a beer,

Cigarettes congest the ash trays
Silted as their smoke-fouled mouths.

Mass participants in drink
These heroes of the commonplace

Anticipate the casual girls,
Timetabled for the last bus home.

Retired Men

They live in a silent factory,
In an atmosphere of truce –
Houses muted, windows glazed with dust.

Today at this spectacle,
The show of the sea, they are alone
Or with families on economy returns.

Exhausted like second-hand settees
Sea noise stuns them,
Continuous machinery.

Unambitious people, they are
Finished with the excellence of skills,
Killing time, they have time to kill:

Green clotted seaweed drifts into the shore.
Their wages stopped some time ago.

Hunting the Hare

This hare is electric. It orbits a track
Floodlit as the bright side of the moon.
Hounds uncoil from traps, intuitive
Experts in pursuit and slaughter.
And these working men this evening

Are the aristocrats of Odds.
Their cluttered living rooms,
The belly-aching, boss-eyed wives who watch
Dull coals collapse into the ticking grates,
Are not a part of this. This

Is the Eldorado of their dreams.
They could return tonight,
Chancellors bearing free gifts for the family.
In a shining sky the full moon's face
Has an image of the hare in it.

Durham Miners' Gala
(i.m. C.S. Hessey, died 1962)

Grandfather told me that Gala Day
How during the days of the General Strike
The miners' band played for the tranquil soldiers
From regiments at bivouac in the meadows;
How out beyond the ends of double-rows
Expectant policemen simmered
Frustrated in their function.

                                        Buzzed by flies
Grandfather drank dark beer, sprawled
On grass green as the blinked sun.

That Gala Day the blue patrols picked up the rowdy drunks,–
Miners, their skin translucent blue as ghosts
Who'd marched behind the colliery bands.
Lodge banners, so silky that they gleamed like coal,
Lay curled up in their mottoes of
Wesley's vision of Methodist peace.

It was grandfather's last time out.
And there I was, helping an old man home.

Remainders
(for J.J. Wells)

There must be hundreds like us now,
Born since the war, brought up
In terraced streets near factory yards
And on expansive council estates.

We were the ones who stayed on at school
In academic quarantine. Others
Took apprenticeships in the skilled trades,
And left us indoors to finish homework.

And we didn't notice it at first –
All the literature that wasn't written
For us: passing an exam
Was an exercise in its own right.

To live like Spartans, think like monks
Had something heroic about it . . .
Now we dress carefully, and at
Introductions in expensive restaurants

Suppress the local accent in our voice,
Not to give ourselves away.
And little by little we go home less
To parents who seem to have fostered us:

We are like those bankrupt millionaires
With our own social-success stories
And personal failures. Remaindered
Fashions at give-away prices.

An Affair of Places

A single rail ticket, its stiff edge clipped
Is my patron saint, a talisman tucked
Into my greatcoat pocket.
Arrivals, departures, topography of distances
I know like the back of my hand.
We enter the tunnel's dark heart.

And beautiful, unmerciful it seems,
Opening on infinity of rails
That all in the end always lead
Back to the same house, the same myth –
A prodigal's love, fidelity of a region:
Minerals untapped in its disused workings,
The potential of its gravity.

A Return to Newcastle

I am up from the South and back to it.
Brown Ale in the cryptic pubs full
Of the lilt of Geordie accents:
A frog-prince back, too thirsty for release,
To truncated ends of terraced streets,
Those old bricked-off perspectives!

Under roof tops hatched like herringbone
Jobless men read paperbacks till dawn
At a loss. Time-served engineers
Done with the sea return to river towns,–
Prodigal salmon spawning in the Tyne
That unrepeatable, one-off gesture.

As a youth on a summer Saturday night
I waited in a shop door for a girl,
Head into the sports page. In those days
A soft curve could draw the eye downwards
Where Grey Street, tawny in late sun,
Defined its limits, its own elegance.

Rooney's Rainbow

And there it was –
A rainbow in Rooney's scrapyard.
Effervescent in the morning sun,
A pick-me-up among
Cast-iron, worn out machinery.
A red carpet of rust petals,
Wilted propellers—the dreams
Of industrial dynasties liquidated!

A crock of hard cash for Rooney
In his made-to-measure dark blue suit
And freckled brogues, a fat Havana
Cigar clutched in his paw.

Singleton

I imagine your father married
The girl late in life, and that
For your matron-mother at the children's home

You were a child you longed for.
You shared in the shift of shared toys
So becoming mild and sure;

Ate meals at long tables
With enough friends for a ship's company.
Even then it seemed voyages

With imaginary companions
You created to confide in,
Who when the small-talk ended were gone.

Though you still have that separateness
Only-children recognise –
An alone, not lonely presence,

In the early morning you find
A strange friend at the wash basin
Who is not a brother you know.

Postcard Poems

i. *The Kiss*

Tucking his nose away across her cheek
Her nose against his cheek
Lips pressing lips—tongue sucking tongue,
His tongue along the smooth edge of her teeth
Her mouth warm as an oven, cool as peach:

An inconsolable happiness!

ii. *Morning Sickness*

A mother-to-be pukes into the pan.
Out of sympathy I do the same,
Woken from a kind of sleep that leaves you exhausted.
It is that time of morning things are most acute.
It's as if we'd lost our sense of humour.

iii. *Telephones*

Their lips are cold,
They do not breathe in your ear.

With digital hearts
Worn on their sleeves
They cannot be persuaded of anything.

Single-minded as cats
They leave you in the end,
Returned purring to their cradles.

iv. *Jugged Hare on Sunday*

It is an odd number,
An incomplete equation
Your absence,–that warm indifference
Absorbent like the softest tissue paper.

Vivid it blooms, tropical vegetation
Sustained throughout a wet season.
Needles of rain are probing
A self-inflicted wound.

Contact is useless sentiment,
Mildewed hope.
On a short walk to the corner shop
I piece it back together, bit by bit.

Dog Exercising Man

He sets it away widely circling across grass
Calling, again and again it comes back

Expecting reward.
When he runs zigzag to throw it off

The dog sticks to him,
Persistent in a hunt for hare . . .

At last it goes loping nowhere
Ignoring his coaxing to play, and he turns

Where his pregnant wife stands apart
With the child that will come between them.

Gipsies

They haven't found a permanent site
For the gipsies: they park on waste ground.

The wiry men have eyes that stare
Beyond any alcoholic daze;

Their kids are scruffy and abuse us,
Or else ask for money.

They are not now like picturesque photographs
Of robust men grinning on clay pipes,

No longer living in caravans
That appeal to our imagination.

That unconstrained happiness
Of a century ago

Has resolved itself into these arguments
With a wife whose belly bulges out her frock.

They appear to do nothing all day.
They are not like us. We do not want to be them.

Some weeks later the Council tipped
Rubbish on their site: they moved on.

Missing

Where did they get to, those reported missing,
The ones who did not send a postcard home?

Devoted mothers forget them making tea,
A girlfriend permits a bank clerk to come close.

Perhaps they found a future life without us,
And up the Orinoco, run a night-club:

Or else spill out life-histories in gin
To a stranger on the night train for the border.

To think of them now would be as useless as
Thinking of a child that died in infancy.

Alone, they stand on a darkened foreshore,
Tropical kit glowing white like bones,

Calling to the mail-boat '–Tell them,
Back at home—tell them . . . '

War Widow

Domestic service was her life
With a spinster in an old house on the sea-front.
Her uniform was black as a funeral dress;
Her room a pre-1914 museum,–
Blue patterned china, stuffed birds in a bell jar.

It reminded her how once she thought
She saw her husband, navy blue,
Slipping through the Saturday crowds,
While on the foreshore pigeon-chested stokers
Passed the time away till pubs reopened.
And how that afternoon,
Going over things again and again,
Her snub-nosed steam iron probed,
A dreadnought through white-pleated waves.

Researching War Poetry

i. *Edward Thomas' War Diary*

While there he was to have observed
The woolly emblems of artillery's fall,
Yet saw signs of spring nipped in the bud.

The men too, already understood
Everything was set for a set piece,–
Preparation for immaculate widowhood.

ii. *Thesis*

She had taken their landscape to heart,
Intimate as any lover
With readings in the poetry.

Later we drove through an England
Sprawling with new town foundations
And proposed future developments.

She spoke so that I took
Earth dug up for drainage
As an intricate system of trenches.

The Done War

i. *The Loss of France*

After France what is there in forgiveness?
We have seen it all in documentary newsreel,
The whole affair miscarried like a marriage:
The English army fallen back on Calais
Leaves its scorched equipment in the sand;
That private soldier who had been a baker
In peace time kneads at soil beside his captor.
And knowing all the reasons cannot help him.

ii. *The Canadian Pacific Railway, 1946*

It could be anywhere and miles
From where we ought to be.
The slow camber of the land,
The estate lit up at night,
A tingling constellation
Too remote to take a bearing.

Marooned,
Among acres of flood water,
We are lost to the world
Dissolving in rain.
My reflection at the window
Is the face of a drowned sailor.

iii. *Rehabilitation*

I was there at the bridge watching gulls
Crashland on the river all those miles inland,
Wondering what it was that brought them up so far,
When I saw you walking down the other bank,
Familiar now in your greens and browns.

Evacuee from a disaster area,
I had come back imagining that time –
Closer than the letters we exchanged,
Further than the freckles on your hand.

Post Op.

No sound beyond the window's pristine frost.
No movement under blankets where you lie,
A Botticelli angel in your nightdress.
An apprehensive cold tingles on
The surface of the hard things in the room.
Dreams manoeuvre beneath the tension of your eyelids.
You ache out of the failing anaesthetic,
A warm faint taste of blood in your mouth.

DAVID CONSTANTINE

'Eyes wide with the moon'

Eyes wide with the moon
He speaks in a tangle of words
How cold her hair was

He would have me imagine the moon
The briars the bedded leaves
A place out of the cold

The cold shines into me
The bright face takes my breath
Withers my warm reply

He will have warmed her hands
A tree he says the branches her cold hair
Among the embracing roots

She will have been drawn into
The moon in his eyes her tongue
Into his mouth . . .

'As our bloods separate'

As our bloods separate the clock resumes,
I hear the wind again as our hearts quieten.
We were a ring: the clock ticked round us
For that time and the wind was deflected.

The clock pecks everything to the bone.
The wind enters through the broken eyes
Of houses and through their wide mouths
And scatters the ashes from the hearth.

Sleep. Do not let go my hand.

Birdsong

Most are sleeping, some
Have waited hopelessly for mercy,
Others even by this will not be stayed.
But we who have not slept for quantity
Of happiness have heard
The dawn precipitate in song
Like dewfall.

We think our common road a choir of trees.

'Daffodils in vases'

Daffodils in vases, watch them daily
For the first touch of dying, even
The blossom you came carrying
Of cherry and almond I will raise
The fire with tonight to see
You naked by, only the tulips
Wider and wider leave them opening
Until their petals fall
In gouts on the marble hearth.

'But most you are like'

But most you are like
The helpless singing of birds
To whom the light happens
On whom it falls
And at whose purity of voice
The skies weep and there is a pause
In all the world before beginning
And before the ending.

'Someone at least'

Someone at least reading about beauty in a room
Above the city has turned from the lamp once having heard
Her step behind him on the creaking board and until
Morning then and until, close in the eaves, birds woke
He was allowed to lie on the narrow bed with her
Under the maps that papered the sloped ceiling
Embracing her freely and planning with her journeys.

Locus Amoenus

One read of the place where the covert mound rose
  Flanked by slopes, and clear water
Issued below for thirst and the excited mind
  And the senses equally were delighted.
One read of that pleasant place in the writers of pastoral
  And imagined its charms scattered over an earth
Less than so beautiful, and thinking never to come there
  Did: and found it surpassed their praises.

Musée du Louvre

These courtiers in a wood have come upon her
Rising before them moonlike in a clearing.
She strikes their eyes, their hands are all upraised
At the light she sheds upon them from her scallop.
Far inland henceforth, deep in the heart's covert,
Closing their eyes they will always hear the sea.

Musée Rodin

They saw the figures of Fugitive Love and supposed them
  Wrought to the condition of subtility
By one another's hands: she streams away
  And the soul may be seen, playing upon her limbs.
The hotel bed was bordered with a mirror
  Where they reviewed those figures, curious
What novel disposition of themselves
  Would lend their evanescence form.

Chartres and Avignon

One could not look through it nor did the light
  From outside enter as light of day
But passed inward in the form of a persuasion
  That love hungers and will be filled by
No dexterity. That was the window of Mary,
  Of post coitum tristis. Waking
In Avignon he saw her beside him sleeping with
  The sheet thrown off, arms and throat
Already burned from travelling. The dirty pane
  Showed a blueness under which the town
With sprinkled gutters foretasted the dust
  And thin shade under walls at noon.

Gothic or Classical

Reading that in the depiction of the female body
North and south of the Alps there were two traditions
By stages night after night in disreputable hotels
North and south of the Alps he examined whether
She approached more nearly the Gothic or the Classical
Bearing in mind from Paris a certain Venus
As far as Florence where a lascivious Eve
Displayed her teeth-marks in the bitten apple.

'The mind then'

The mind then seems to become the burning point
  Of the other senses, when by day
Arches are seen and one's delight converges
  At their tips and down the aisles, and when
In darkness are corresponded all parts having stiffness
  Actual or potential, likewise
All declivities and entrances and more are devised
  And the mind then is the glass, burning.

Rodin

Upon his dictum 'Dessiner c'est connaître'
  Gossip put a lewd connotation
Saying that master of the essence and forms of women
  Entered the place his pencil had depicted.
Oh do not leave it to gossip lewdly to imply
  Our certainty that through the foolish penis
Exact and loving knowledge comes. To that point
  The cognisance of all the senses runs.

Renoir

He answered: 'With my penis.' Let us not
  Imagining the inconveniences of palate and easel
And dismissing Bullhead as an unmanageable tool
  Jump to the conclusion that he meant it figuratively.

STEPHEN DUNSTAN

Black Earth

feels good on the knuckles when you punch it
firm yielding fertile earth, dark
where a drop of blood
grows into a man
or a petal spreads out
into yellow acres
a seed blossoms
into blood-sown poppies.
earth magic
so good in the hands.

man observing landscape feels alien

The landscape seems too indistinct to care
laycr upon layer of lovely light
green upon green,
the bunched trees dark with early winter:
the mauve cloud surrounded sunset
spreads great wings and sinks.
I cannot bear to watch this beauty
and turn away as though in pain.

At my feet there lies a dead vole
its back pinched by the jaws of a cat:
a pet, who killed in sport.
Crime on crime on crime
am I rejected because of these?
Or is it that, among so many,
to the landscape my solitary form
seems too careless to be concerned?

War without End

We dig ourselves trenches and stake out flags,
fence guns and handcuffs linger in the mud;

waiting for ambulances, red cross food:
dull tin-boxed manna but it's all we have.

We're dug in for the winter now, a lifetime playing cards
the rattle of imagined bullets is only rain
but we make what sordid glory we may
from the ordinary drudge of daily digging.

Gold-miners in a peat bog, our native guides
must be laughing at us somewhere:
to suffer all this for a dream of riches,
our homes abandoned in searching for this ditch.

Empty House

The armchair leather has split
with waiting for former occupants
the walls have shed their skins of paint
birds sing crazily in the hallway
broken windows snatch the April sunlight.
Somewhere upstairs
the scratching of rats sounds
nervously welcoming
like the hesitant music of Spring.
Damp clothes rot on their hangers
wardrobe doors creak open
and in the corners of abandoned rooms
silken threads soften the shadows.

Caravan

We go among dust.
Our fins and gills and wings
have gone, along with other powers,
other skills I cannot numerate.

We go among dust now
and drag our feet.

Beside the one road left open
over the steppe, which with erosion
is becoming desert,
lie the bleached skulls of sacred cattle.
I kick them aside: what use are they now?
I can't undertand why
we carried such things so long.
We are at least wiser now
about such things. Before us
the sun is deep red on the horizon,
like an open gorge.

October

Thank God for the wind that shakes the leaves
off a tree, and does not let them hang on, and on,
forever going browner with decay.
And the snow or slush that covers and disperses their memory
into the soil: which eventually loosens the hold
that old things have upon the world.

If only it were not so slow; still
more lenient in this than other lands,
these English winds so patient and unwilling
to really shake them down: the long delay
through October, November, almost to Christmas in the south
the old leaves hold on, and threaten to suffocate the trees.

Night Thoughts

I turn out the light inside the room
opening my curtains onto the darkness.
Streetlamps discover and conceal
aspects of the world they neither see nor care for.
Behind dead brick walls the dead leaves pile:
without hope, without remorse.
I sit back gripping my glass
and slowly sip the dark liquid.

I shut my eyes and the trees shiver,
the hush of wind and rain falls suddenly;
small animals split between fear and wonder,
from floods and the fresh wet smell.
I listen and wish and stop thinking at last:
the earth slows down, my blood pauses.
This wine is the tears of blind men
the rain on the window a sybil's lament.
Somewhere out there I hear echoes of myself:
half in pain, half possessed.

'The marshes are evil'

The marshes are evil. They stink of petrol
pumped out of blazing vehicles, abandoned
skyscrapers half sunk in the sludge;
and by night the light of bonfires jumps
from black puddles up to the star-blown sky.
Across the marsh I hear the sound of chanting voices,
sparks flit and hiss above the desolation:
in the mud are the imprints of bare feet.

These civilized noises were not made to last:
the insect song in the lamplit forest
will continue long after the lamplight's gone.

As I lie in the semi-dark listening to the vast
meaningless noise of inhuman night
the spit and crackle of fire seems welcome
whether in a homely hearth against winter
or out across the marsh among the gods.

'Tombs of the unknown dead'

Tombs of the unknown dead lie out like white grass,
meaningless friendships buried in stone;
while red ants anxiously run over my desk
among coffee pools and torn manuscripts.

All this work and all this time: after dark
the arc lights sweep the barrack windows,
restless men roll over in their sleep
imagining a breezy night over green meadows
now full of white crosses while the mud bleeds
in reparation and the long, slow clouds
swallow the grieving moon.

Spartacans

So here we are:
three days ago the rains came, and since then
they have washed us almost all
away, the water like applause
on the glass, stars
baptised into hailstones, water
for our bodies and air for our lungs.
Choking, it has washed us clean,
our bodies wrinkling
like past fashions,
withering away until we are left
stretched uprights, narrow gouge-faced
Giacomettis, tapering
wasp-waisted sculptures, till here
we are:
plain voices calling
across the sands,
along whose shifting crests like fish
our last dissolving vestiges
are crucified.

And then there was

and then there was Davie.
round face
blue eyes and blond headed
coarse hair like rush matting,
brushed backwards:

smiled often, seldom laughed.
'andsome fucker me (he said it himself)
and talked to you only when he knew you well.
he moved
with the slow momentum
of the half-compelled.

*

colours stay in the mind
according to shape:
the roadside jumble of leaves
soon shuffles into
a simple pattern, and so slots
in the memory
like enamelling.
and behind the leaves, faces.
and behind the faces, chains.

*

and then suddenly they're gone:
Davie, the faces, and the leaves;
grey predominates,
and thin bushes
seem delicate, too delicate to be
everlasting.
the hedges can be seen through now:
in a couple of days the whole world
has been exposed.

*

colours stay in the mind
like enamels in silver,
like leaves, like
faces in the air.

'What am I writing about'

What am I writing about when I am writing
about nothing?
I am writing of the spring,
spring flowers, and their futility.

October, and the world was burning down
around me: yellow-orange bonfires
rushing up the mountains; but now
the winter bones are bleeding green again
and the blossom will pretend once more;

to whom does my song belong when my song belongs
to no-one?
It belongs to the birds,
birdsong, and its futility.

I believe in stolen oranges

Flowers in a Japanese bowl
reach for an artificial sun
stretching with exquisite grace
dead
they make an elegant pattern
to prove this living ugliness.
Their educated lines portray
offence at my physical stare:
used to contemplation,
the dry hands of monks;
abstracted thoughts
recoil from my sweaty grasp.
But I am not such an artist
I could never pick flowers
to build little dead gardens:
pleasure
is to me the taste of rough-skinned oranges
stolen from an orchard
and eaten, lazily, under a tree.

DESMOND GRAHAM

Remembering the War

I.

Clear blue, perhaps;
it came down, soundlessly,
as I remember:
time to rush next door,
upstairs, see
through the binoculars

or was it gone already,
just blue, and smoke
above trees to the left:
time to run a hundred yards
turn onto the common
cross the rutted grass
and see the farmer
pulling out the pilot,
one of ours

or just too late
(how can I remember?)
a small crowd
already round the fire
well back from the blaze:

I had run to meet
something, excited, certain,
this, my first memory,

looking back, I imagine
the white-hot airframe
was the element they fought in,
brought down for us
to understand: I cannot
remember what happened
cannot even recall the heat.

II.

Stuart was my friend, my best friend
until the new gang won him.
'Catch this!' they said he shouted
lifting a mine. It killed him.

I accepted when his mother told me
his body was not marked.
When the rest came back from hospital
I asked them nothing.

III.

I have this dream. A plane, effortlessly through the blue, turns and falls towards me, out of control. I run, but it makes no difference: each time I stop I see its course has altered: lower and faster it is heading exactly where I am. Familiar now, I recognize the sequence, even through sleep. I run, and crouch in panic, hide, and run, knowing that if only I can keep the dream within its pattern I will wake.

IV.

My mind still clings to the brick
at shoulder height on the corner
of Ludwigstrasse and Schellingstrasse,
pockmarked. The young girl told me,
there, in 1968, a student died.
I pointed to the wall: 'That tracery?'
'Oh that,' she answered. 'That
was British high explosive.'
When she'd gone, I hoped by fingering
each scar my mind could make contact.

Two blocks away, I lectured;
Amalienstrasse, where the Gestapo
beheaded White Rose idealists in the street.
I looked through windows they had opened
to throw pamphlets, and saw traffic,
students, bookshop and my own reflection.

V.

'The heat from the sides of the burning buildings was so great, we made for the Rhine. Some of us just bathed our bodies, others jumped in. The Lancasters turned, flew low along the river, strafing the water and the banks.'

'I have turned'

I have turned and kissed you asleep
and lie here to your breathing, a seal
afloat on darkening estuary water.

I pass the glittering fish which the ebb-
tide brings me. No more disturbing the water
than great birds curling on currents of air

trouble air, I slide to the river's bed,
searching, turn as a bird turns, touching
only the water yet darkness rises around me.

I remember a child at a pond-side, easing
his arm through the clearness of water, reaching
through mud so gently and yet the pond clouding,

forcing his arm, back and again
to the mud, closing his eyes to feel
through the slime, and finding there nothing.

You stir. I close my eyes and float on the seaward
current, looking for sleep before you awake.

The Parthenon Frieze

How many hands made this? Hands
made it, all of it. It is not
the permanence, not the outlasting
of time, but the moment when
someone stuttered his chisel

through stone, smoothed the
surface with his hand and
felt the folds of cloth
or feathered manes of horses.
It is not the permanence but
the moment the stone is seen.
Now in the distance between
my eyes and that stone
is no distance. That it
survives me is only for other
lives, other eyes to let
that charioteer more girl
than youth, with crossed bodice,
pleated breast and two deep
channels of skirts, enter
the eye. The art is alive
only in me and I live it.
It is not the stillness of art
nor its permanence but
a living of beauty as
we make it.

So we must
live art, making living into
art, as Turner has shown
us the sky but only we can
look at it, daily, even
without his intensity, live
what he cannot live. So
in turning a corner, watching
her push back her hair,
seeing the bones of a
face, each movement, looking
on rooftops, the snow as it
feathers the roofside, the
birds as they lift up their
plumage and so briefly
ruffle back into shape: to
live such moments and find
there are others, in looks
and talk, growing from
what has been lived,

new moments as candle-
light catches a feeling and
shares it.

                Why does
the Parthenon frieze which
I touch with no more than
my eyes, fill me with feeling?
Not for the beauty it is, the
story I cannot get right, the
reason they made it, but for
the hands which felt in give
of the marble as the chisel
moved through it a presentness
they had and I
am the only possessor of.

Portraits of the Artist

I.

He is a marine biologist
afraid of water: pilot
who cannot stand heights:
pot-holer, helmeted, swathed
in rope, waving a flashlight
through afternoon sun: Edgar,
survivor, left with the last word,
the balance of his sentence
proving it lies.

II.

He takes the vessels from deep water
guides them through sandbanks, shallows,
all they must pass to harbour. He

is the man who knows each coastal current,
rocks, tides and depths enough to anchor.
What would the sailors do, knowing the ocean,

knowing the wild waves' running, if he
could not bring their great ships through
the charted channels, safe to port?

III.

'Defend me friends: I am but hurt'

He is Claudius not Hamlet, not Polonius,
the king, flawless in design.
Humour him and he will bring you
Rhenish. Cross him and your part
is written out. Fools he only uses,
it is the wise man he drives mad.
In private he will win your pity.
In public he will show the sense
of balance others lack. Magnificent
arranger, it is the chaos
which surrounds him pulls him down.

Isabella in the Mirror

There was no one there, really
there was no one there as Isabella
stepped from the heavy coil of clothes
around her feet and hesitated
by her bath. Through all the reticence
of childhood she had had no thought
of how her body bloomed. Now
her eyes could not believe the beauty
that they saw: hair touching
tiny shadows where the faintest
tracery of veins spread from shoulders
travelled to her breasts, the slightest
down along each gentle line.

She paused, her wonder opening
to loneliness, loneliness to shame
as if Susanna only saw the elders
in her own reflected gaze.
She turned, moved to the bath-edge,
arms vainly angled as though
awkwardness could take away
the truth of what she'd seen,
could hide the pain which told her
she alone had seen it.

Rain

Under the sycamore's umbrella
the heavy summer rain
at evening
is its sound,
only a shower
out of sunlight
slanted across the wash of clouds,
the rain its weight
meeting the leaves
and birdsong
opening stillness

I would find love for this
with you
or thoughts of you,
would love the stillness
rain on leaves encloses,
with memory maybe
of snowfall
enclosed
or under an umbrella
catching the sound of rain
apart from the rest of the street

or find love
in the circles love can discharge

looking outwards,
each echo of love
a new sound,
this tree, its canopy
newly green,
its green flowers
seen for the first time

but I am here
with only the rain on the leaves
heavy
its weight
and its fall,
and nothing in me

as all over the landscape
trees take the weight of rain
and no more,
turning it into the stillness
of sound

and my face takes only the palpable
change in the air,
my ears the rain,
my eyes the glistening trunk,
each leaf so securely
feeling the weight of the rain
and nothing in me
is needed,

the emptiness under this tree
filled with no more than the tree
and rain,
is a bell of green
with its soft green sides
open,
it sounds through the gaps
between leaves
extending stillness
through the whole evening
the wide open landscape,
long after the rain.

The Choice: Two Riddles of Feeling

I.

I am the one who kills with good intent.
I am warm clothes against frost;
A fireside against cold; a shady tree;
A bench; a turning point; a story
With a happy ending. I help you
Sleep, and when you wake make breakfast.
I am the arm around your shoulder;
The hand within your hand. I am
Comfort, and you call me shelter
As I slowly kill.

II.

I am the one who gives you life.
I am naked, feeling every blow.
I am your open eyes and the blinding
Sunlight. I am your fingers
As they split with cold. With me
You are sleepless, yet I bring you
Nightmares; when I close your eyes
It is with pain. I lock thighs,
Tie hearts, separate and break them.
I am exposure and you call me living
Till you meet a sudden end.

Afterwards

She is the girl in the Victorian painting
playing the piano to a background of trees
the afternoon sun brought from the garden opposite:
the sun moved past her picture
leaving her lilac dress a shadow
cast back through blackened glass.

'I am lying stretched out'

I am lying stretched out on the floor,
dozing. With a rustle of clothing,
someone bends over me; our warmth

makes contact: my weight, shoulder,
arm, side, hip, flows towards
that contact. She does not meet me.

It is as if snow fell and stopped
a tenth of an inch from the pavement
then more flakes, resting their weight

upon snow, and none of them touching.
I press against air, pour into impossible
distance. She does not reach me.

Death

A clasped shell grained with ochre
down its matching smooth grey walls
but empty.

A stone glittering as soon as dry,
veined gold and blood-red, ungiving
in the hand.

A bird tarred in a caul of oil left
as if the sea had let it slowly slither
from its hand.

A sea falling from its urgent lines
of rolling white into the listless
momentary shallows.

A Set of Love Poems

I am writing a poem from what has happened;
I think of the image of a furnace
I think of walking you towards it
I open its door,
I think I turn away,
I cannot find the next lines;
I leave you in its heat
I know I have brought you here
I need the heat yet cannot face it
As you do. My poem fails.
I meet you on the landing,
knowing I must not hold you,
knowing I can close the furnace with my arms;
looking past your shoulder I hear you say
'Your face is warm from the fire.'

*

Thinking of the photograph, I see puffed clouds,
blue sky, sunlight and grey fence of
winter trees masking the snow-white hillside.

Returning home I find the negative, dark
clouds, grey sky, a line of white-
spiked firs above a blackened hillside.

The photograph I gave you, cherished, shared,
the negative unwillingly I take from the family album
and hand you this, the latest picture.

*

You showed me the bottom of the river
I laughed and pointed to the clouds:

You showed me a heart torn by anguish
I patted your hand:

You opened your mouth wide, shouting
'See what's outside!'
I fastened the door.

You took me to a black lakeside, said
'Look! The water bubbles like pitch.'
I made tea, turned to you and said,
'I love adventure.'

*

I rebuild the sandcastle
cross half the beach
for a single piece of driftwood
slap it against the melting walls
and watch the waves lose force;
checking the tide's pace
I run barefoot up sharp shingle
dig my fingers deep through sand
and lift my boulder:
staggering to the sea's edge
I search the wash of water
and find nothing there;
the boulder empties its weight
into my arms.

*

After the most enormous noise
and then slow-motion time
I veered through space,
almost blacked out;
I sit, finding I am not dead,
fearfully check legs, arms,
in growing hope, my neck,
start to trust, to accept
all I most wish to know,
and know, slowly,
nothing can save me
from leaving my wreck
to look in the car I hit.

*

Only you could write the poems
of the place I cannot reach:
with a single gentle push
I slipped your boat from its mooring
back into that water

you had known since childhood;
I wave to you as your small hands
struggle with unwieldy oars,
your body stiffened for balance;
I see you clearly
but your eyes watch the skyline,
wait on weather as little waves build;
I stand at the water's edge
knowing that if you founder
I cannot swim;
I speak to you
and the wind blows away my voice,
I shout and my words are jumbled echoes
of a single word you speak.

Living on an Island

An island is a sea
you walk on, where impossible
infinity of space is brought
to earth as weather:

the sea is not our element,
land's security deceives–
our time is less than rock,
far less than sky:

dam-builders, sowers of spear-grass,
knowledgeable planters
we must be, seeing
the land's erosion:

our time at best is seasons
and so few,
more truly wind on a day
of grey sky, rain

and momentary plains of blue
where we ride
tethered to the wind's control
driven by its freedom.

PETE LAVER

Placing Sensitivities
(for Bob White)

The emotional melange
bursting out over the
brittly realised landscape –
a boiled egg
blurbing its delicate shell
when the top is severed.
You asked for the mystery
of my emotions
to be revealed;
for the tantalising hints
that slink among the crags
or wink between night-clouds
to be brazen
as the summer sun
or oozing breakfast egg.
But the bitter wind
or the mist that falls,
the single raven
or the broken bough
are felt as much, and give
as much diversity
as the heart that trembles
or the voice that, longing
or in gladness, calls.

Two Wood-Gathering Poems

1.

From John's Grove
I look across the Lake:
pigeon-wings and
ragged clouds hanging rain
at two thousand feet.

Green lawn rises

to Allan Bank,
lit pink under a dark sky
by a tower of arc-lights.
In this wood the bracken's swaying,
the beeches hiss.

  Ken Russell's filming over there:
  Wordsworth's hand stays
  on his sister's tit;
  Coleridge is laid back
  charting his way through desarts.

  The house is that much
  smaller than the hills it
  burns among:
  cameras and actors' eyes,
  the director's mouth, on fire
  under roofs
  under rain that crosses valleys
  from Sergeant Man to Scandal Fell.

I twist and swing upon
a dead oak branch
while angles of the Lake's face
fuse or clash.

  Thomas Ashburner winks
  then nudges giddy Wordsworth:
   'A woman can count stars
   longer than you can count
   paving-stones.'

2.

Mother Nature it's a risk
I take with you
recognising our empathy.
In Banerigg Woods it's
growing dark
and there's cloud in hollows
above Nab Scar.

I stop and think about you:
wind from the North
along the Rothay,
silver side of the alders moving.
I think about the way
you dress yourself
and hear you speak,
not the voice I'm speaking to
(the wind in the birches
the river running into snags),
but like a voice
behind the voice I talk to
on a telephone.

Up there on the ridge
cloud whispers.
Down here the bow-saw
squeaks through wet birch.

Cragfast

It's not celestial light I'm missing:
that's always here
a minute's walk away
brightening the larches
and the new beech leaves,
particularising stones and lichen.
It's the bodily weight
of one more job to be completed
one more manuscript to sift
someone else's poems and revisions
to worry over.

This unintelligible mood:
conflicting fragments of anxiety
frustration and desire;
anger seething for release;
solitude become "an issue";
children's moans that
tighten nerves.

Maybe there was a time
when every mood
was easiest whim,
but now I tell you
here's my bluntest knife:
complete the job
I've started on my heart.

Moment to moment to live
tightening up muscles
& arteries
breath trapped
in a library.
Tangle of black branches
and the sunlit rocks beyond;
love, like the breeze
up on that rock,
thrilling and relaxing every nerve.

Rydal Mount, 1840

The fire blusters
and the clock ticks.
My wife's in bed
and my sister
wipes dribble from her chin
and *hums* a scottish tune.

Time was,
the wildness,
ice hanging from crags
in clustered tubes
and I looked through an eye-hole
in that ice
towards Far Easedale Moss
where you moved
among stones
which collapsed
for our rites.

The clock fusses
and the fire clicks.

At Blintarn Moss

Death brought me to a place:
the becks running into quagmire,
sedges, green moss,
oily at the roots;
mist seeping down,
one raven utters
as it flies among the rocks.
Here and there in the bog,
islands, turf-covered
and scattered strange
shapes of juniper.

Lungs ache from the effort:
the mountains sending back
my cry of WOE!

Woe!

Speeding
(for Wilko at 31)

I'm beating shit
out of a balcony rail
while you do splits
in mid air
down below me.
Rock n roll at its best
is when you forget
everything.

A thousand masks
flip across your face,
fear and loathing
and sublime stupidity.

The punters are jumping
on one another's backs
and exploding catherine wheels
of beer.

Down by the control panel
I lose intensity.
Speed. Quick bursts
of gibberish and true
confession
followed by hours of quivering
white walls.

*

Ear drums still hissing
I'm driven north,
rolling numbers:
desolate Stretford
then the M6 runway
back to moonlight mountains.

A hundred miles south
and wasted,
your central nervous system's
coiling tight.
One small mirror,
a razor blade,
and a nose
sniffing for details.

Holding the Impulse

I watch a sheep
cragfast on Nab Scar
turning and turning
in the wind
that freezes my hand
tight to the stick
I hold.
You try and follow
where I point

to see the animal
whose only relief
will be in falling.
The steep wall in front of us
is perfectly smooth,
not random beck-stones gathered
and by some miracle
held fast, but bricks split and
levelled
to check the mountain's
faults.

The sheep circles
and a raven spins
on the strong cold Helm winds.
O my daughter
what whim
will lift your eyes
from the beauty of that wall?

That Mythical Poet

in Brazil
who drilled a hole in his head
with the appropriate
domestic appliance
to rid his brain
of its mechanistic
front lobe
and get to the rear
of Pure Imagination.
All he retained
was the image of a blue chasm
a fracture in the vapour
the deep and gloomy
breathing place of
one voice roaring.

JAMES LONGWILL

My Father

2309252 Sergeant James Longwill
Served overseas: France 7.10.15 to 13.6.19
Singapore 27.8.39 to 14.2.42
POW (Far East) 15.2.42 to 8.11.45
Discharged on ceasing to fulfil Army physical requirements.

A few miles
below his hillside grave

ships. Iron
and sulphurous air.

There I think of him
and of others like him.

Between them and England,
as between me and him,
I say it in that Burmese word

Sokiebiami, the desired earth.

Bobby Arnet
(1790-1869)

1. *Ayresome Village*

At fifteen
I wore a man's jacket
and steadied the plough

the horses
dragging it,
the earth curling away.

The work-shaved leather
of bridle and belly-band
were my tackle.

Working in fields
before first light
was metalled on walls.

Ditching, drain-laying,
that night
nursing the sick beast

while the wind blew the rain
like a wet tarpaulin
slapping against the byre.

And the evenings
cheeks warm with
the flame of winds.

Leading the horse,
its slack puppety trot,
down the field paths

to Ayresome,
the little houses
by the river.

2. *The soldier*

At eighteen
the wars
ended all that.

I was
pressed into
the King's shilling.

I fought
in Spain
and at Waterloo.

Discharged in 1816
I walked back north
found my family evicted

land sold
mortgaged to neighbours
who bought us out.

Got no
start at
Yarm hiring-fair.

That winter
I tied sacks
about my feet.

3. *The house*

Their children play
there now. We made
its small, red bricks

from field-clay
dug in autumn,
left for the frost to break.

Next spring
fired
in the kiln.

We moved there
from the old house
our great-grandfather built

with stones lifted
out of fields
and that rusty stream.

Like that old house
I blacken
in the weather.

Grow
harder and darker
in the face.

4. *Cholera*

1802
floods all winter
harvest failed.

Beasts felled and salted.
Two years, rain all summer
and bad drainage, harvest failed.

Next spring, our faces like lanterns
white lights
weak and sickly in fields.

Three days
I watched our kid
die of cholera.

Instead of
the dark rubble
of the bowels

he passed
nothing but
watery shits.

His tongue
dried and cracked
like old leather.

By autumn
stone over him
'In the eighth year of his age.'

5. *Their farm*

They've done well
since the coal-field
opened in Durham.

1836 the slaughter-house
full of their beef
for the Durham market.

And now Middlesbrough
fills with Irish
they go over to dairy.

I see the beasts
led back
for milking

steam rising
from the raised masonry
of their heads.

I see the dairy's
scalded and
salt-scrubbed wood.

The tools
in the barn
scythe, flail, spade.

Their wooden handles
grained and shining
like a worked palm.

I say the names of their pigs
Yorkshire, Gloucestershire
and Tamworth Gilt.

6. *Greatham Creek*

I read the Bible
in my house-boat
by the estuary

the flat land
of water
where the tides crawl

unbroken by
the long planks
of the waves.

Here by the sea
and bitter water
I will be clean.

I go to it
over dunes
where the sharp grass cuts

then over
the wet
bird-printed sand.

I catch fish there.
They move like smoke
under water.

Other days
I collect driftwood.
Go to the woods

to kill vermin.
For six crows
I get three parish pennies.

7. *From the prophet Isaiah*

Now they are
building staithes
and lighting buoys on the Tees.

Furnaces light
the night
in a gale of flame.

I hear
the sound
of hammers

and the
plate-breaking
noise of trains coupling.

Where once
the light
lay down in fields

there are
buildings
with darkness in them.

And from coal and iron
will come
the building of cities

never gracious
at the voice
of thy cry.

The Hawk

hovered
tautly girt on the wind;

concentration
impacted under its frown.

When it
dropped

rooks
snapped out of branches

flew up
in a din of gargled caws.

Before dark
I saw it fly off

loggy,
replete with kills.

I heard no sound
but the small thorn of its cry.

Blackamore

1. *Field Notes*

Flints
like teeth.

A pit
full of unstringed bones.

A causeway
like a dried-out river bed.

A crow's
rusty gutturals.

Tumuli
starring the map.

A rampart and ditch.
A quincunx of stones.

2. *Urra Moor*

Drained by
bronze-coloured becks

it surges
up into the sky.

Its growths
are primal:

algae
pullulating in pools;

lichen
riveted onto rocks.

Left to
the moor

dead sheep
are soon a shipwreck of bones.

3. *The Shepherd*

The sky
an estuary of light

and the
first stars

already
drifting like continents.

Before dark
he must leave the moor

to the larks
buoyed up on their air-jets.

To the
lamb's cry

trembling
under the stones.

VINCENT MORRISON

The Schonau Express

Nine hours of boredom in the darkness.
Humming the only shabbat song we know
as the crippled express rocks us into Austria.
In the thick fog of our carriage, shabby families doze.
The children fight and scuffle down crowded
corridors, or listen to the bristles sprouting on
their fathers' chins.

Norma's dream is a blurred travelogue
of tattered maps and orange groves;
summer igniting the singing globes of fruit.
We travel lighter than the rest, rolling to the
monotonous pant of steam as the engine strains
towards Bernau.
I stretch out wet fingers to touch her lips;
blood has caked on this steamy pane, brown
against the blinding glare of frost.

I ask one guard our time of arrival.
He looks up from his grimy clockface of playing cards
to stamp 'Who needs to know?' on the back of my wrist.
In all the confusion we've forgotten the name
of our destination.
Norma still sleeps under my grey trenchcoat,
her skirt is melting against her thigh.

The Polish Rider

1.

Winter is our mountain
a hill is my horse.

She nibbles raw onion
and sips rainwater;
flecks of gunsmoke, a grey smudge
against her trembling bag of bones.

2.

With the prince's likeness
tattooed on our nipples we
sit in saddles of sheepskin,
watching the pilfered icons
being loaded onto covered wagons.

O to leave the servants scratching;
naked and scabby, arguing over thrones and brocades
like swivel-eyed lizards at a swarming pool.
Their royal eagles on standards of crimson thread
are unfurled to blanket the trodden dead.

A bishop's priceless bauble rattles in my quiver.

3.

Into the sun I'm astride Nina
the dangerous white mare;
her eyes are a fist of wild berries.
My body slowly eases into her rhythmic lumber.
She carries me gently,
sidestepping the slush.

Our Lady of the Nettles

Ash scatters, like the gang of truants
rolling marbles on my stone.
Are their bones as fine as maidenhair
or greener than this tidied plot?

The priests gulp down diluted rum,
measuring the silver trail of God as he
clings slug-black, to their powdered brick.
Are their bones as fine as spider-thread
or greener than this rug of moss?

God's coming, wrapped in death's cobweb
warms to a bible's pin-drop in the trees,

or times itself by the tick of a crow.

Approaches my whore's blood
rushing the cemetery as stones rattle,
shifting the dust of men underneath.
And
were their bones as fine as my barbed stems
or greener than my monthly blood?

Gwen Pullen

Sand undresses to a locket of wormbones and is black
through its polished flint the tide's scraping
of a drain like a lover's nail down a naked back.
Here rain shaves the clay from a poet's white cross,
on slopes above his wave-shouldered cabin of words.
Below this trembling shack, a salt thread of foam
slips away from anglers like the first milky bubble
of children from a man.

Dancing under the skeletal stilts or limpet-sucked
struts; Gwen Pullen gets drunk on brine,
sleeping with lobsters in the bullstails of weed
and crackling noose of eels.
Her split pods shimmer in the pier's lens,
then shape to nipples of rain on spider ruins.

Closing Time

1.

A derelict in furious rain
stranded in the concrete no man's land
between bald verges and a ditch;
the last lived-in house on Trimdon Street.
Stripped of lead and copper wire
its facade sanguine though blow-torched
the colour of a diseased bitch.

Auntie's cottage had grown sour on us,
four cells rank with balm.
Her fortress had become a shrine to
                                        Christ the King.
Tiny orange flames winked beneath a pastel
                                        Sacred Heart.
She courted God, as errant daughters do.
Good Friday my brother groused: 'Jesus, we'll suffocate!'
as if our breathing ballooned a polythene bag.

2.

She craved pomegranates not communication;
three singing knobs of ochre and puce
became tender and mute under Pyrex glass.
Sally sedated, propped on turtle-green pillows,
gaudily rouged like a pantomime dame.
It was her privilege to ignore baldness,
declining the red hairpiece and a blonde.
Trolleyed after communion to the last cot in the ward
next to the swing doors and a German TV.

In Memoriam Michael Smith Killed 1880

Out of the pit
and the nagging of winders;
dripping brine, cage gates crashing
behind his eyes.

Men pedalling drunkenly home
(vertebrae blue-buttoned against the frost)
to the gust of starlings in treetop slums.

Mist. Purple clover skid-marks the slag pyramid.

Herring-bone struts
criss-cross each roadway and catacomb.
No tarmac. A litter of mice pellets,
snails of slimy shag and nibbled bait crusts.

Christ's beads of blood
spray in orange sparks
from a blue hymnal of fern fossils.

Your flame, like a glow-beetle dies in the dark.
The taste on your lips
the salt of Margaret's damp kiss;
turning to scalding piss of ponies crushed
under the goaf's white splintered skull.

A desperaţe intaglio
in rust on your water bottle:

dear margret
were at a prayer meetin
tonight i'll be in the hands of god

In Sickness and in Death
(i.m. Robert Lowell)

1.

The wind is a waterfall in the trees
ghosts pummelling buckled slats;
a fool's moon smokes above Montessori.
Rereading *The Hallmark of Horror*,
a dozen numinous homicides.
In our motley warren of quilts
chills turn to swelter of fever.
Two paracodols that taste of lye
still swirl like a snowstorm
in the vodka tumbler.
Overhead even the floor sighs
as it is walked upon.

2.

Outside us, the clutter of ephemera
and slivers of immortality.
The carapace of a silver-fish

pressed between acts of *Twelfth Night*;
ticket stubs, 'that article' too,
taped above the stone fireplace.
A portrait of my sober hero
part Aegisthus, part Agamemnon
three tarred fingers to his brow.
Cogitative, though divorced from reason.
Rapacious, even under saintly gilt and glass.
'He was unyielding like marble,
penetrating like English mist.'

Henry's Dilemma
(i.m. John Berryman)

Henry plotting lay, the scarlet
song of Crane (play-wise?)
He thought of rising but
alack it was so cold.
'The blood has frozen in my pen'
wrote Henry his Latin patroness
—late of Botteghe Oscure.

But what of his public fans?
'Dey will yo to go on, persevere!'
shrieked Mr Bones.
He wd swig and muse.
Ah shaggy Henry could count his
lovers on the fingers of three hands.

The Incas

Bound by coarse hemp, these
puppet-skulls wail. To
  his ancient, wizened
  forehead, glossed smooth by
    the wash of floods, a
    boy presses four gnarled fingers.
      In the ruins of an
      Inca temple, the bones of

two petrified Indians, once
buried under a million tons
   of alluvial mud. Mother
   and child, with their pet
      a grinning mongrel bitch oss-
      ified by centuries of
         'natural disaster'.

The Eve of Abdication
(from *Nacht und Nebel*)

Jenever was a fever-killer.
Maryke said, by comparison
Gordon's was small beer. Then darkly:
'Tomorrow is not the holiday you imagine
I'll drive to Apeldoorn instead.'
All night a battalion
tensed inside marquees.
Taxis, nose to tail
bleated round bollards
of monestial blue.
Late trams trailing groundsel
sparked on the stucco,
grumbling like spavined mares.
I was fellated behind buckled slats;
Spinoza brooding opposite, appalled.

LAWRIE WALKER

Landscape

here is a wooden stool
a curtain for modesty
a reasonable bed

here a stocking dropped to the floor
can be studied
impressions may be recorded

there is no innocent work
for those without keys
but here you may imagine occupation

without windows
geometry is pure
as a blank horizon

here you may learn to pray
—a reed in a fog
—a stick adrift on a lake

only

the wind blows from inside
clouds flow from your eyes
bells ring out the absence of time.

Head (Christ) XVIth Century

And there is a droplet
ruby
tracing his cheek. It leaves no trail:
a rich red rounded mirror, small
as a pearl.
Thorns also, smooth ebony,
disappear
in the brow's bright edge,
into that white untroubled sea.

He is thinking of bad apples.

From his left eye
another perfect globe,
leaning on stillness
as a glass cherry.

He is thinking of pigs,   clifftops.

Exuberant with brown wheat
his beard
as a stilled storm;
his mouth defenceless as a girl,
flushed and full.

He is thinking of waves,   loaves,
the ready cave;
the hole where God was and isn't.

Now it's all begun
it doesn't seem real.

Expert suffering
by an old master,

not as it happened,
perhaps as it was,
through centuries
of contemplative gathering poise.

Old Master

sick with wealth
I followed

blessed with lingering disease

having hammered the moon
to a metal sheet
as protection from dreadful starlight.

blotched
pitiful
malignant

uttering old prayers
I stumbled

in my vision white thighs
the rhythms of the sea

a salt trembling taste
a scent of fish

her face out of focus
her hands blurred
. . . . . . erased . . .
erased
as Tara's Halls.

what if I trample
the swan's cracked neck
the madman's vomit?
rage is all gaiety
when the fiddler carries a gun.

sweating
itching
distorted
I pursue

rich with illness
my old limbs shudder
like a dog in the rain

no longer upon my skin
do I feel
the deep blue bruise of health.

no walking naked now.

stones fall from my mouth
and pretend to grow.

Eloise

blessed. ripe as the harvest moon,
as a manuscript rarely coloured,
richly bound.
in drifts of incense I sense your breath
cloistered within your hair;
your eyes, sustained as Chartres' rose,
reveal your hooded dreams,
my chancelled lady.

enfold these hands that hold the host
as snow on moorland
in the clear glass of night;
a plain pure song.
the river of wind is in the pines,
the clouds are in pilgrimage.

*

so you say, locked tight
in metaphysic ecstasy.
if I lower my eyes to my own pain
it's to babies and prams, the crowded bus,
arguments in shops.
saints in darkness, chaste and torn,
adrift in the alleyways of prayer,
raise images that love can comprehend.

accept my letters and my trust,
leave me this wooden bench,
this chosen stall;
my office and desire
within Christ's keep,
my darling.

Seaside 1943

sea coal on grey beaches,
thin children play.
bath scum

clutters and slops,
the horizon tilts awry.

lead ships smoke in convoys,
slow procedures on the concrete floor;
the sky alarmingly empty
as silence drowns the day.

urinous pillboxes,
ragworms, urchins,
fags,
towels,
torn underwear;

a temporary landscape
held by the war's delay.

mothers click and fidget,
boys float sticks, drop stones;
girls stare at stains
drifted in through shallow pools.

money is scarce,
the men being away.

Skiddaw

down there the caravans,
the valleys laid for high tea,
a colourful variety,

but up here
edged onto the rim
white smoke drifts from a constant war.

the ice goddess has grey dugs
and sharp, pitted thighs;
her shadow cuts across stalled waves.

comfort cannot manoeuvre
among broken bowls,
bin spills of scree.

small birds
gust
as ash in windy chimneys,

a heavier squall of gulls
litters the undercloud;
their screams drizzle and sway.

from the path
the tarn
offers black oiled bread,

closer,
the entrance to a drowned ceiling
whose cliffs descend to a limitless sky

where men crawl
head down, trailing ropes into hell
with peculiar gravity.

War Effort

I.

there goes grandma's railing
into Karl's left leg.
when his government is wailing
he can jig.

Karl's grossmutti's grate
put two red holes in Herbert's pants.
as the politicians supplicate
he'll dance.

II.

when the god
came down from the machine
in answer to the people's fears

no one was surprised to notice
the steel helmet,
the zinc zip grin.

women kissed unfamiliar mouths and flags,
husbands offered bed and breakfast free
as the turret swung round ablaze

with victorious wreaths.

Reasons for not entering

there are many ways not to enter
the open spaces and natural paths.

  a door clattered against the wind
  banging the frame
  but did not enter;

  a droplet dimpled a silver net,
  nippled, swelled,
  and entered.

you pressed me in the heaving night
to blindly touch and breathe our way;

  I was too set on going through
  to enter.

MIKE WILKIN

The Intrusion

not zen
persimmons
misty
on a page

but two
apples
on a
chair;

a silence
not wanting
us,

our voices
flounder
like bats
in daylight,

the room
demands
we leave:

apples,
and weeping
dust

Autumn

and leaves
drop on
the lake
an old
man skims
stones off

At the Start of Day

from darkness
of shivering trees

sparrows tumble
to standing water,

tilt into
gleaming stiffness

shatter the mirrored sun
with their burrowings,

flinging gold
across one another

jostle around
a shit-slippery rim,

then fat
with wetness

clatter
to a streaked fence

to preen
and dry,

and say
their song

Metamorphosis

a girl not beautiful
feeding park swans

stabbing beaks
leave blood
maul her fingers

with the given bread

a weeping hand
floats slowly
to her mouth

and eyes
flit across
the lake
finding sanctuary
in a mist
of far trees

she is beautiful

Moment

forest pigeons
clatter out of
high branches
off across
the valley

rabbits bolt
to dark havens

finch songs
fray abruptly
to sour
scolding

  heart in mouth
  frozen by guilt

apology
for a
snapped twig

and urban
clumsiness

in still penance
waiting for quiet
to begin again

Disturbance: 1 a.m.

a scream flares
in darkness

beds groan

startled feet
slither across
cold oilcloth

rapid prints of light
identify a street

the kicking stops

lover departs from lov

the girl shoves blood
from her face
   will keep silent

he'll marry the scars

For Jean

tranquil
aftermath
of loving
as late winds
rouse leaves
among stars

embrace
of lips
and skin
words mouthed
on closed
eyelids

with your
departure
moths and
darkness
haunt restless
windows

scent of
your flesh
lingers
soothing
the bruise
of parting

smoothing
your presence
from pillows
unfurrowing
tangles of
warm sheets

a long
loose hair
of you
falls glinting
against
my heart

tidebirds
startled off
midnight sands
splashing
across wide
silence

Haiku

1 Trailing cloak
Of the moon—poplars
Spare and silent.

2 Grey-voiced gulls
Exiled to bitter air –
Lake ice glistens.

3 Snow falling
Against sunlight—against
Swaying rooks.

4 Lake a dark silence,
Vast assembly of stars –
The moon absent.

5 Chained boats nibble
The island—crows scrape
Over docile waves.

6 Swans caged by jutting
Ice—spitting
At the hand of rescue.

7 Darkness gags
The skylarks—sky and moor
Silently mingle.

8 Cattle floundering
In fields of white mist –
Clatter of piss.

9 Crossing the wide moor –
Seven raindrops
Find my face.

10 Football in the park –
Goalposts
In blossom.

BIOGRAPHICAL NOTES

PETER ARMSTRONG: Born 1957, Blaydon on Tyne, and brought up there. Studied Philosophy and Literature at Sunderland Polytechnic; recently married.

GEORGE CHARLTON: Born 1950, Gateshead; educated on Tyneside. Has worked in further education since 1973, and is now teaching at Newcastle College of Arts and Technology. Co-organiser of Morden Tower poetry readings.

DAVID CONSTANTINE: Born 1944, Salford, Lancashire. Read Modern Languages at Wadham College, Oxford, where he wrote a doctoral thesis on the poetry of Hölderlin. Has lectured in German at Durham University since 1969. His first collection of poems, *A Brightness to Cast Shadows*, has just been published by Bloodaxe.

STEPHEN DUNSTAN has divided his time in recent years between Hexham and Oxford; now in Peking. *Tarot Poems* (Bloodaxe Books, 1980) was his first publication. His second book of poems, translations from the Chinese of Ma Zhi-yuan (Yuan dynasty), will be published by Bloodaxe in 1981.

DESMOND GRAHAM: Born 1940, Surrey; studied at Leeds. Has lived in Newcastle since 1971. Other poems have appeared in *Poetry and Audience* and *P.E.N. Broadsheet*; some broadcast by the BBC. Published a biography of Keith Douglas in 1974, and edited his *Complete Poems* (1978) and *Alamein to Zem Zem* (1979)—all three from OUP. Poetry reviewer for *Stand* since 1975.

PETE LAVER: Born 1947, Watford. Studied at Newcastle University; Ph.D. on Henry Thoreau's anarchism. As editor of the (now defunct) magazine *Ashes*, he helped link the University with poets such as Pickard, Harrison, Pybus, Caddel, and Alistair Elliot. Moved to Grasmere in 1976 where he is now the librarian at Dove Cottage and part-time tutor for the Open University in Cumbria. His drawings have appeared in many magazines; published work includes *Guillotine* (Pig Press, 1974) and *Pete Laver's Anarcho-Marxist Fun Book* (Vertego Press, 1975).

JAMES LONGWILL: Born 1947, Hartlepool; brought up in Middlesbrough. Has taught English at schools in Bradford and

Stockton-on-Tees; also a tutor for the Workers' Educational Association. Poems broadcast by the BBC and published in a pamphlet, *A Man's Jacket* (Pig Press, 1977).

VINCENT MORRISON: Born 1952, Sunderland, and brought up there. Has spent the past year on the building-sites of Holland. His poems have appeared in various magazines and anthologies, and in *Two Poets and an Illustrator* (1974), a Wearmouth 1300 Festival publication. *The Season of Comfort* (Bloodaxe Books, 1979), a pamphlet, was his first collection.

LAWRIE WALKER: Born 1947, Gateshead; left at 17 to work in London. Lived for a year in a Benedictine Monastery, then studied at Manchester and Exeter. Taught English and Drama in Hull; now lecturing in the Department of English and European Languages at Bayero University, Nigeria. Married, with two children.

MIKE WILKIN: Born 1945, Stanley, Co. Durham; brought up in Newcastle. Studied English and History at Newcastle Polytechnic. Poems published in numerous magazines; has given many readings, taking part in reading tours of Sweden and Denmark. Published his own pamphlet, *Winterset*, in 1969. Now sells books; lives in Cullercoats, near Whitley Bay.